Tiny Infinities

Blake Wells

BookLeaf
Publishing

India | USA | UK

Presentation by *BookLeaf Publishing*

Web: www.bookleafpub.com

E-mail: info@bookleafpub.com

ISBN: 9789357444330

First edition 2022

DEDICATION

To anyone who can relate

Just One Tiny Infinity

a moment
a breath
an emotion

written down
captured
preserved in time

at the will of its
creator
no moment is
finite

tiny encapsulated infinities
sometimes crossing
sometimes parallel
but never dying.

they.

they.
an identity
a statement

four letters carrying
the weight
of my existence

it's just
a word
a pronoun
a label

I am so much more
than my words
I am so much more
than my pronouns
I am so much more
than my labels

Passion

ink spills
damp on the page
releasing
internal sparks of passion
illuminating the world around you

write to
      feel
the spilled ink
creating words you can't speak

write to
      create
an infinite spark
exciting minds of those not yet born

write to
      release
the passionate fire
burning hot, white flames inside you

This is Not a Love Poem

This is not a love poem.

it can't be because that
would require me to
accept the feelings I've
fought so hard to suppress

prisoners locked up
behind bright green bars
sometimes gold, yellow, or grey
it depends on the light.

This is not a love poem.

it can't be because that
would go against every
rule handcrafted so delicately
by exhausted fingers

three meals a day
showers three times a week
no fighting, no arguing

lights out 10pm no exceptions.

This is not a love poem.

it can't be because that
would mean I've found
someone who accepts
my imperfections

brick walls plastered
together so thick
they break bulldozers
without so much as a flinch

This is not a love poem.

but it maybe it is because
I think I've found
someone whose heart
beats in just the right tune

to lull prison guards to sleep
to make rhymes out of rules
to whisper walls into oblivion
and to make love poems out of nonsense.

6am

When the moon
in her eternal beauty
reaches across the Earth
with welcoming arms
stretching around your soul.

When the stars
their billions of familiar faces
wading through pink seas
with promises of hope
illuminating the world around you.

When the sun
in her constant strength
checks in on you
through green curtains
with a touch that breathes life.

In that moment
when the rest of your world
feels unsafe and confusing
the moon, the stars, and the sun
will hold your spirit safe.

How to Say Goodbye

You said it through tears
  dusting the pages
  of the letters you wrote.

You said it with your voice
  every pause and short sigh
  loosening our tethered souls.

You said it with your eyes
  their shifting glances
  never quite reaching mine.

You said it with your hands
  a ghost like presence
  once so familiar.

You said it with your lips
  their kiss no longer
  stretching across my face.

You said it with your heart
  beating to a song

that I've never heard.

13

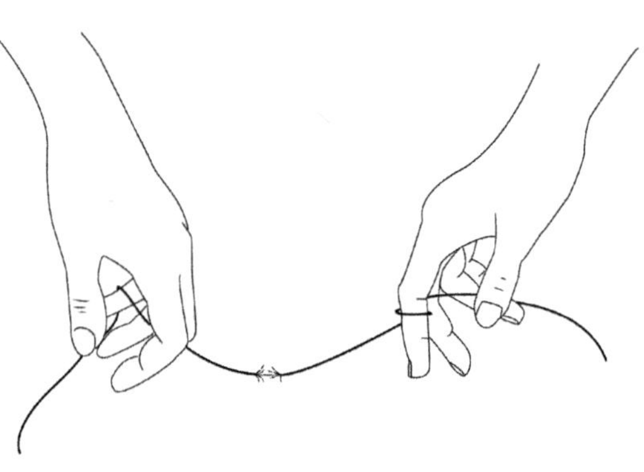

Kayla's Poem

I knew
  that night
warm bodies clung together
I was
  scared
to feel
to want
to need
you changed that.

to the point of no
  return
I fell.
you caught.

together we
destroy, to build
  again.

I am a part of you

I am the first one you came out to,
when your voice cracked and faltered.
I am the first one you think of
when your world becomes a black hole.
I am the first one you look for
when your thoughts take on marathons.
        I am a part of you,
        an extension.

but when the day comes
that my well dries up
will you still reach for me,
long after I cease to offer
a comfortable grip?

black. gel. fine tip.
smooth. no smudge.

                see me
                like I see you.

0930

Sweaty hands twitch and tremble
searching for something – anything –
to grasp tightly as if existence
could slip away at any moment.

Outside our eyes strain to see
only relieved at the rusty truck's
whining growl that sends
silhouettes dancing across front doors.

Breathing out peppermint ice
into the late September air
we were not prepared
for the winds shrill screams.

A crackling fire sends
summer camp smells
delivered eagerly to
nostalgic noses.

Short panting breaths force
aching legs to halt
at the perfect moment
just as it was planned to be.

Rehearsed lines
rolling across the backs
of eyelids while steadying
breaths waft through the air.

A trembling voice nearly
lost against the howling dogs
asks the question we've both
been eagerly waiting for.

With bated breath we circle
infinitely around the black hole
of anticipation that waits
for an answer.

"Yes".

Do you feel it too?

Children laughing,
babies crying,
dogs barking,
trees swaying,
the world is existing
while distant eyes
are handcuffed to screens
monologues and moments parading
recklessly through winding streets
do you feel it too?
the locked doors
and barred windows
shrinking walls
and numbing silence?
300 light years out
circling black holes
and empty space
      where is my mind?

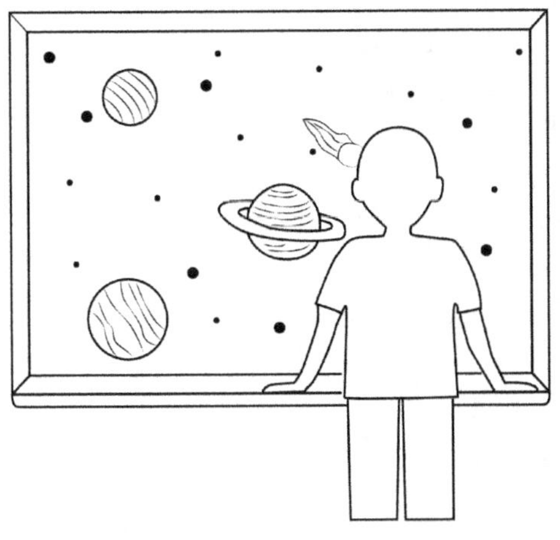

Young Love

Come lay in
my bed
let me pull
you closer
to me
by your waist until
our bodies intertwine
our lips find their
way to
each other's.

Come lay in
my bed
let me hold
you so close
to me
that our breaths
become one
our skin
share warmth.

Come lay in
my bed
let me kiss
you until

your stomach
tangles itself with
butterflies
and my mind
dizzies in a
swirl of ecstasy
at the touch
of your lips.

Come lay in
my bed
let me caress
your skin
until the night sky
swims in blurs
of pink and
orange as the
sun whispers
over the horizon.

Come lay in
my bed
let me grasp
you tight enough
that two
hearts beat
in symphony
against warm flesh.

Come lay in
my bed
let me love you
enough that every
crack and crevice
carved out of
your young heart
by the cruelness
of humanity
would be delicately
smoothed until
all memories of
mistreatment are
washed away into
darkness.

I love you
I love you too

Future

I'm lying in bed
the cold morning air
summoning chills across bare skin
you're sound asleep
covers pulled to your chin
I watch the steady rise and fall
as you dream of other worlds
and I dream of our future

I always struggle
when people ask
"Where do you see yourself in five years?"
because I can't imagine
growing up or being independent
but as I sit here and look at you
I can't stop picturing a future
where I get to wake up before you
so I can take in every detail
before stumbling blindly
through our kitchen
to fill two cups of coffee
just to see your smile
as you take that first sip.

This is the future I see now.

i'm sorry

I am 10 years old
you're standing above me
cigarette smoke
          engulfing
my entire body

you look like a boy
girls don't dress like that

I know
it's meant to be
a joke
but the words
still scratch over open wounds

I am not
a girl

I want to
          scream
back at you
my voice
a machine-like hum
fading into the air
it doesn't matter anyway

I am 10 years old
you're standing above me
what I
        feel
doesn't matter anyway

final thoughts

sinking, submerged
life in ripples above me
blurry words whisper
songs of despair
a disenchanted siren
begging for death
choked sobs reminding
of suppressed pain
threatening a relapse
a time traveller forcing
the past into the present
       take a breath, please.

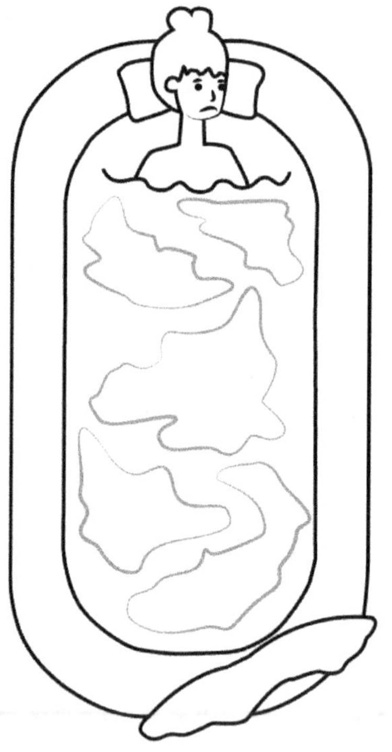

Reflection

Every day I pass by
familiar faces
now strangers to each other
we once shared memories
created secrets all our own
discovered the universe
found love and felt heartbreak
danced and sang
to songs only we could hear
we built cities all our own
    we were one.

Every day I passed by
I watched us grow
    and divide
two faces staring blankly
at each other, never touching
always critical, never loving

Twin souls
now barely tethered
I don't know who you are
    anymore.

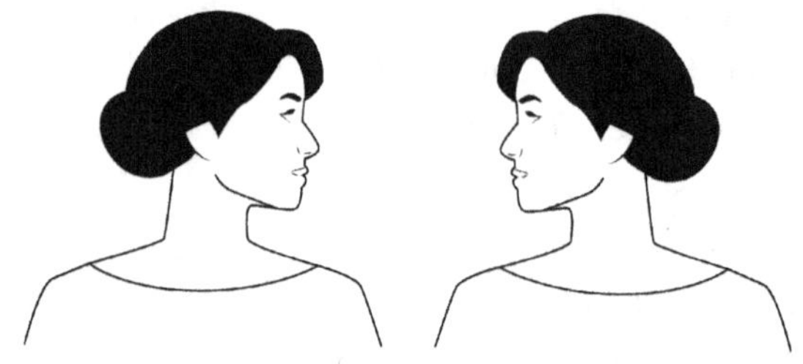

anxiety

you told me i was worthless
i was a mistake
i was easily forgotten
and never enough
you told me i was wrong
made me question myself
and my abilities
you told me i would never
achieve my dreams
that i wasn't smart enough
or pretty enough
or creative enough
you told me to be quiet
to know my place
to listen and never speak
you took away my innocence
you took away my spark
you took away
who i was
who i am
and who i could have been

so how do i move on?

Therapy

Cement feet dragging
across flooded plains
tomorrow promises light
three steps up with a two-step ladder
reaching through black holes
searching for answers
to a test with no questions
stare into open wounds
a past that's never left
reality that's never lived
       search within.

A Letter to a Kick-Ass Kid

four years old
life is about army men,
baby dolls,
dinosaurs,
and stuffed animals.
simplicity and freedom.

you are not yet prisoner
to the stares
and the second glances
to the whispers
and the awkward questions
you are not yet prisoner
to your own mind.

ten years old
life is about friends,
boy bands,
homework,
and the cute girl down the street.
simplicity, freedom, and shame.

though they are not about you
the comments still linger
stale smoke clouded
deep in your mind
save them for later
for now just remember
who you are is not normal.

fourteen years old
life is about perfection,
hiding,
pretending,
and hoping those feelings will go away.
confusion, lies, and shame.

racing heart, restless legs,
and dissociation when you're around girls
tangled thoughts, shaking hands,
and worry when you're around boys
staring blankly at bathroom signs
there is no place for people like you
not yet anyways.

seventeen years old
life is about transitions,
self-discovery,
life plans,
and acceptance.
determination, advocacy, and shame.

the stares and comments have caught up
no longer clouded deep in your mind
you've been taught since childhood
that who you are is not normal
that there is no place for people like you
working through this takes time
you still have so many years
until you figure yourself out
until you find your people
until you feel whole

if everyone is the pilot of their own life
then you're a fucking astronaut,
the spaceship
ground control,
and everything in between

labeled boxes will try to contain galaxies
but you are so much
            more.

YOU

www.ingramcontent.com/pod-product-compliance
Lightning Source LLC
Chambersburg PA
CBHW070609160726
48003CB00005B/2192